LIMBIC
IDEOLOGICAL DIMENSION

A BRIEF DESCRIPTION

VISHAL SHARMA

notionpress.com

INDIA • SINGAPORE • MALAYSIA

Notion Press

Old No. 38, New No. 6
McNichols Road, Chetpet
Chennai - 600 031

First Published by Notion Press 2018
Copyright © Vishal Sharma 2018
All Rights Reserved.

ISBN 978-1-68466-380-4

CONTENTS

ACKNOWLEDGMENTS

This brief description puts light on the discovery of the fourth dimension in the political spectrum called the limbic ideological dimension.

I am grateful to my parents, family, teachers, friends and all my loved ones for supporting me in every walk of life.

Authoring this book would never have been possible without their continued love and support.

ABOUT THE AUTHOR

Vishal Sharma completed his B.A.LL.B (Hons.) from the Himachal Pradesh University Institute of Legal Studies (India). Currently, he is pursuing his Masters in Public Policy, Law & Governance from the Central University of Rajasthan (India). He has contributed a number of articles in various journals, books, and blogs. His research interests include International Law, Political spectrum & Public Policy. Recently he and other like minded people started an organization called the *Limbic Movement (For more log onto www.limbicmovement.com)* which is the world's first ideological movement centered around a civic & social organizational sphere furthering the use of the limbic dimension in the fields of Law, Public Policy & Social Work.

INTRODUCTION

Ever since the French Revolution ideological divide especially on the basis of the political spectrum started and thus the limbic comes as a dimension of the political spectrum to diverge the divide into another possible direction. The political spectrum currently consists of major dimensions referred to as the right wing, the left wing and the centre. The thought process in the centre mostly pertains to reasons and their research coated descriptions, while the right wing functions through creating an atmosphere of resonance by explaining a particular stand in as many ways as possible and the left wing is more focused on providing resources through the power of reason. And differentiating from all the above mentioned dimensions is the limbic, which includes the working on the attainment of resources and making sure the process is in line with their values. It is a combination of the right and left terminology in one sense and is entirely separate from the centrist ideology. The concept came into plight after the thorough study of a psychological theory called the Whole Brain Approach which studies the brain and the way it runs through its four major systems [Right, Left, Cerebral (Centre) & Limbic] and although the political spectrum is similar to the psychological theory of the Whole Brain in its typology but it does not have this fourth dimension, and this is a discovery the study tends to unravel with the hope that this would eventually lead to the formation of the ***new political spectrum*** having four major political dimensions. Not only that, the emotions it will seek to systematize would have to be governed under the ***global legal order*** because it may be true that because of man laws exist but instead, it shall not be perceived to be false if I say that because of law, man is existing and in the future may continue to exist but the survival is getting tougher and so are the increasing complexities of laws, as in one region an act may be a crime in the other it may be an incentive, in one aspect killing someone may lead to a death penalty in the other aspect it may fetch you an award, in one law a state claims to forward peace in the other the same state legalizes violence. A person is given a right to self-determine his representative on the other hand not to self-determine his region or language, and in this divide, the two main antagonists are the municipal and international laws. As individual law provided by nature states that a human being has the right to defend himself, which led to coming up of laws and institutions in the first place and when the group increased, the local or community driven setup came up and then with mammoth increase, the provincial and national setups came into being and in this globalized era where boundaries seem to be unwanted, it would be fair to say that in fact, the globe needs a global setup with a proper global law at place and it is only then this ideological dimension and the movement centred around it would flourish.

LIMBIC: AN ALTERNATIVE TO THE LEFT, RIGHT & CENTRE [DE FACTO EMOTIONAL FRAMEWORK]

Birth of the New Political Spectrum through the Whole Brain Approach

Ideologies are "groupings of contested political concepts" (Freeden, 1996:82). Those contested political concepts are described through a system which classifies different political positions and perceptions called the political spectrum. The political spectrum currently classifies the right, left and centre positions and perceptions. But through the application of the whole brain approach in the political spectrum, a whole new system seems to emerge which not only adds a fourth element called the Limbic to the political spectrum but also leads to the formation of a whole new political spectrum.

Discussing, the *Whole Brain Approach*, it is a psychological approach which studies the four parts of the brain through its divisional modes.

As stated in Figure 1, the Whole Brain approach describes the four modes of the brain and the various approaches it works upon to create change in the mindset of others. Firstly the Cerebral Mode which works through a mixture of reason and representational redescription, it focuses on not only having facts and research behind the change but also explaining the change in as many ways as possible.

Secondly, the Left mode works through a logic oriented organizational aspect, focusing on making sure that people have resources as well as a resource system to sustain it. Thirdly, the right mode works on the integration of interpersonal and emotional aspects to change mindsets and lastly, the limbic mode which works through organizing the interpersonal and emotional needs in a detailed way and form.

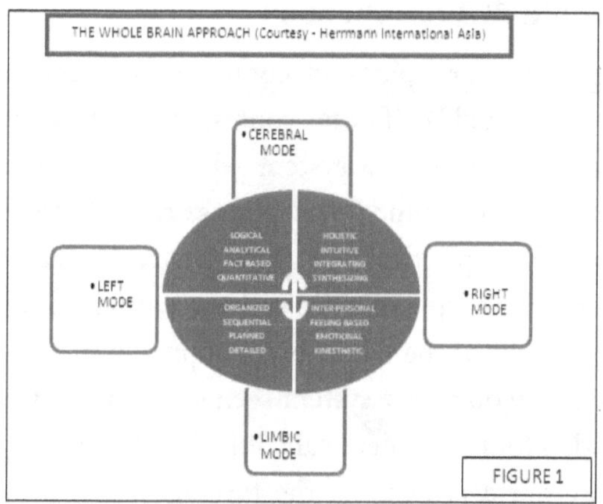

Now coming onto the *New Political Spectrum* and as to how it gets its birth from the Whole Brain Approach, the approach points out modes through which change in mindsets is done, which when seen through the eyes of the political spectrum showcases how ideological backing develops within a person which when further combined with other people in his category leads to the broad classification on the right, left and centre vectors. But wait, the whole brain specifies four modes and on the other hand, the political spectrum only revolves around three classifications. This leads us to the limbic, which when added to the political spectrum will not only complete the relation between the Whole Brain Approach and the Political Spectrum but would inevitably cause the formation of a New Political Spectrum.

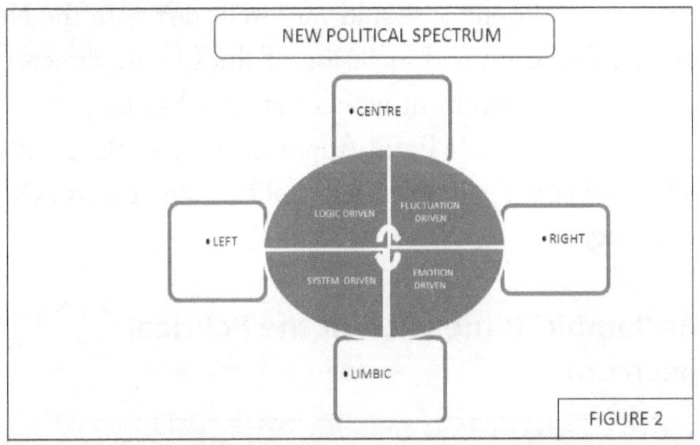

The New Political spectrum would then consist of four major dimensions Right, Left, Centre and Limbic in close scientific psychological relation with the Whole Brain's Right, Left, Cerebral and Limbic. The linkage is proved as follows:-

The Centrism's balanced approach of doing politics is resembled by the analytically logical and at the same time holistic and intuitive cerebral mode. The leftist politics of furthering reason and targeting the handling of resources can be seen in close proximity with the scientific and organization inclined left mode. While the rightist politics of integration of emotions and forwarding of resonance closely resembles the right mode which is more inclined towards fused feelings and emotions. And lastly, the limbic ideology focusing on integrating resource based emotions has a relationship with the Limbic mode which runs on a feeling based organized setup.

And as Azmanova analysis suggested on us witnessing "an end of left-right ideological vectors" (Azmanova, 2004 : 282) and the erosion of the centrist thought, the start of a new agenda of politics should very well start with the New Political Spectrum and inclusion of the Limbic dimension in the political spectrum which not only has the scientific backing of the Whole Brain Approach but also the practical backing of how the limbic socio-political sphere has existed since long.

The 'Limbic' Dimension of the Political Spectrum

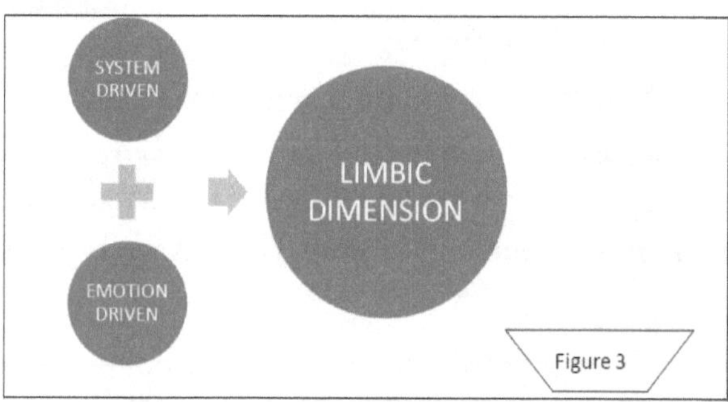

The Limbic emerges at a time when both the Right and the Left are confused as to how to tackle the mass uprising where either it be a right ruled state or a left ruled state, the crisis has erupted from below, and the help of the centre where both sides take a deviation is also not doing any good, thus the need of the limbic is what will transpire as with forms of resource neutralization it also has forms of emotions attached to it and even if the right and left seem to be the dominant northern and southern forces the limbic cannot be denied. A lot of challenges are also faced by the three ideologies in the political spectrum. In the left side, the decline of the trade unions and the labour unions is of the utmost concern. On the right side, the increase in modernity bypassing traditional values is a sign of huge worry. Although, both accept the merging of the two platforms to a greater or lesser degree with the centre which leads them to be either centre-left or centre-right. On the flip side the centre is cobwebbed in the Third Way platforms and also the radical centre phenomenon. Thus the Limbic seems to be the only answer for now as in this post-ideological society people want nothing to do with the party system driven by the three major inclinations but they are willing to forward their perspective on issues which deal with their inclination on specific issues which effects their resonance relating to resources and rewards and thus the limbic seems to be the way out in this concern.

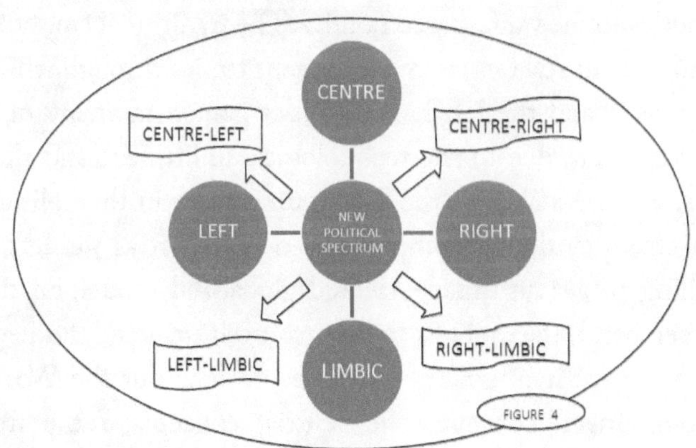

Let's understand the issue in lieu of the Kashmir dispute. The mainstream parties there can be seen as the centrist forces, factions like the Jamat-e-Islami can be seen as the rightist elements and JKLF can be seen as the left element and if the limbic gets infused then the voice of the people would matter, which will swipe away the fluctuation of the centrist sentiment in the people, then a UN-mandated referendum would wipe out the leftist sentiment in the people and further the reintroduction of ceremonies like 'Tajomouj' (Foster Mother Culture where when a child was born in a Muslim family the first breastfeed was from a Hindu mother and when a child was born in a Hindu family the first breastfeed was from a Muslim mother) and circling a propaganda on the Hindu-Muslim unity may very well lead to the swaying away of the rightist thought. And thus, Limbic may very well be the new kid in the block which runs wild on the system. And there will be a day when a faction will be called limbic or right-limbic and left-limbic. As this will lead to a new surge and connect the resource-based politics to the value-based politics. The traditional emotions and the old style resource attainment tactics through which the right and the left based politics gained momentum is phasing out, due to the technological upliftment and thus one can see a slot for the limbic dimension in the political spectrum as the current scenario demands it as the left is failing to get an urban-oriented globalized model, on the other hand, the right is failing to catch up with the neo-liberal pace it originally forwarded to take out the World Communism concept. The centrist concept of the free world is also failing to live up to the hype it created leading to the formation of democracies especially in the third world countries and with this pace of globalization which may be seen as government mandated or citizen mandated creating a rift within all three political approaches in the spectrum, the only way to come out of this mess seems to be the Limbic. As globalism seems to be the new key as defined by Stager it is a new thought system which 'sustains asymmetrical power structures in society that benefit a loose heterogeneous and often disagreeing global alliance of political and economic forces (Stager, 2005: 26) and from global feminism to international populism, all can be tackled by the limbic. The Limbic is more than a postmodern thought. And if it is agreed that citizens can no longer be motivated to be part of a certain ideology but mind you, the limbic is different as here the combined efforts of the citizens lead us to the notion of having or setting up an ideology. Because it can be agreed that motivation can finish but can the emotions? Is what I forward.

And as stated by Azmanova, on us witnessing "an end of left-right ideological vectors" (Azmanova,2004:282) and the erosion of a left-right continuum, it may very well be the New Political Spectrum and its Limbic dimension which leads a new agenda of politics in the 21ˢᵗ century and beyond. But the new agenda will not blossom until the emergence of neo concepts stop within the two wings and the centre.

Simultaneously, it differs a lot from the reactive Right and Left, the Limbic is the action-oriented dimension along with the centre and the time may come when the descriptions of the two may, in fact, lead to them being the elitists in the New Political Spectrum, meaning the limelight would shift from the left-right divide to the centre and limbic dominance, and they will take over the left and the right due to more rationality in the combinations they profess.

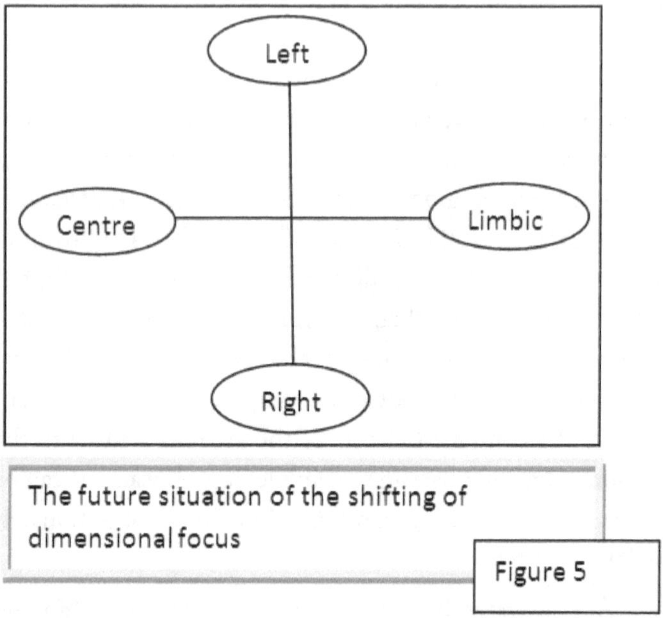

The future situation of the shifting of dimensional focus

Figure 5

Conclusion

Studies have tried to churn out molecular ideologies from the traditional spectrum but the focus was never shifted to discover the fourth part. Although the previous use of the dimension has been there in bits and pieces, no attempt was made to discover it in entirety and stress was always put on revisiting the old one. Though some hybrid ideologies may have taken a spot in the already existing nomenclature, but this dimension would help us rise above the issues of identity, religion, and economy which have become more important in the politics of the contemporary world. The Limbic is not at all a resistance theorem and nor is it a counter-ideology, it is a part of the political spectrum which cannot be laid to rest by redefining the right and left dimensions.

The limbic is an integral part of the political spectrum and it is here to stay.....

GLOBAL LEGAL ORDER (MANKIND IN SEARCH OF A GLOBAL LAW) [DE JURE LEGAL FRAMEWORK]

Introduction

The provinces can constitute a federal nation-state in the eyes of the **international law** to what I will refer to as **inter-national law** then why can't nations constitute a federal global state in the eyes of the global law. The global law is somewhat different from inter-national law, most people regard law as a set of rules created by state institutions, now in the nation state's perspective it may be public law which relates to the constitution, criminal codes etc, or civil law relating to contract and tort and when the term nation is substituted with the word inter-national, birth is given to public inter-national law which governs the territory and its population plus civil inter-national law which sets its eye on sovereignty and government related aspects and criminal inter-national law which has nil say currently.

But laws inter-national in nature are not laws for the entire world as in the literal sense the word stands for more than one nation which in the actual sense is a reality. On the other hand even if they are regarded as laws for the whole world then also ignoring inter-national laws and structures have been part and parcel of the inter-national game when it comes to the conflict between two players, but that can't be said for say national laws which in majority cases cannot be ignored by provincial players.

The Core Argument

This coquetting mindset should be changed to a united front and if this method is to progress with absolution, then a legal framework for the whole world seems the way out. That is why the world needs a law which works beyond boundaries, systems, and theories and in fact it can be a law of the global state governed by the world government which would cover the earth and its people, places or things, and would not be subject to conventions, covenants and other consensus-building measures where most nation-states differ from each other. The areas to which that law stretches may not be that vast when it comes into existence and can include aspects like environment, conflict resolution, human rights etc; so that justice as fairness prevails without having calculations of addition or subtraction on regional or municipal levels.

Then with time, it can be extended to every legislative, executive and judicial system. Say from having a global law of media coverage to a global law on corruption to global taxation & company laws or say global education laws. It can redistribute income and resources and the nations can be dealt with on merit rather than diplomatic fronts. It can intimate in the future a great system which can kill the existing ideology based tourage to a full idea forwarding reception, and invariably when fused with the concept of having a World Government which would be the rightful fifth layer in the Governance module consisting of the local arena, the provincial arena, the national arena, the inter-national arena and the proposed global arena. Such a law then will be the one which dictates the terms and rules the turf, from having a common global code which will not be something out of the box, as if a nation's population can give to itself a constitution and inter-national population can talk about abiding to a common charter than why not a common code which when implemented through a world legislative body can bring together the global citizens.

Invariably, this type of order will in phases eliminate defense budgets, spying costs, fencing costs and human rights violations in lieu of protecting boundaries. The global legal order will start a type of world regime where nations would be federations within the world state, in the same line of provinces being under the national and local bodies being under the provinces. And the trafficking of law by nations and provinces for gains either on the issue of self-determination or protection of territories would get wiped out.

From secessionist wars to race and colour based oppressions to ideology-driven wars all would sink in the abyss of the global law, whose main objective would be utilitarian and solving of majority claims and at the same time not solving them. And the prime examples in this context arise in the Morocco-Polisario conflict over Western Sahara to Indo-Pak wars on Kashmir to the Jerusalem territorial problem over which Palestine and Israel are at loggerheads. In simple terms, a world without all this can only come into existence when we substitute law for no law at all on the inter-national front.

The politics which runs through the veins of these measures would be tackled in the name of giving self-determination and the economics would be centrifugal, thus creating a decentred in a centre and a centre on the decentralized landscape, in fact making the grey prevail instead of a white and a black. As everybody traffics on its own profit then why can't somebody stray on its own loss, As Hobbes made the concept of the contract to do away with the war of all against all then in this day an age when nations are on the move of either one versus all or for that matter some versus few then, for the protection of all the nation-states and its people why can't the concept prevail and if Rome came into existence after coming together of the population there with no one being considered above or below on racial, cultural and other parameters and USA can come into existence after coming together of states voluntarily, then why can't one believe that all the nation states can become one, but considering the divisive elements in both Rome and USA which caused a lot of headaches one should be cautious and thus the global law comes into the picture as it can help solve the division.

If Vico's New Science can forward a theory of nations arising from mythical beginnings why can't a global actual law forward a global order, question over the national and inter-national laws is not a problem but the question over they being the only laws is where the problem stands, as major players are given the walkout and minor players suffer. The UN and its conventions are not the problems but the mechanism with which they are progressing is where the problem lies in the actual sense. If provinces can be dragged into federal courts why can't federations be dragged into the world court and that can be achieved only through this mechanism at place. Wilson may have forwarded in his fourteen points to the noble idea of enshrining nation's self-determination as a principle of inter-national relations and the idea of the League of Nations, but the word subjugation missed in the self-determination principle and in the idea of the League, the concept of general association of nations was where the problem arose from and the UN can also be put in the same league when it comes to implementation of laws and keeping in mind the problems and complexities the common purpose aspect in the global legal order can help tackle the existing norms. Say if today we are in a world federation and the UN is at the helm of affairs, then we surely need an institutional legal framework which the UN does not have, it neither has legislative powers nor does it accurately and effectively separate the three powers.

Thus global law is nothing but reality in our thinking, what happened in say Bosnia & Herzegovina, Lebanon, Sri Lanka as to what is happening between Russia & Ukraine to what is transpiring between India & Pakistan to the Rohingya Crisis in Myanmar to say the Israel-Palestine conflict; disagreement has affected almost every level of government from the formal rules and procedures that structure and constrain the political process to the actual implementation of those rules and the decisions that result. It is also the best theory for handling the republican & democratic divide. The bottom line for all is that nation-state authorities are having limited ability to persuade the people to support the public initiatives and this is leading to a gap from which the costly resources are being churned out in unreasonable numbers and thus are leading to the depletion and simultaneously are causing their un-repented destruction. Global laws seems the only way out to forward world peace and justice and with the increase in the ultras in both the right and the left, the law and order problem will surely erupt as now also the divide is deepening the divide more which if not brought under the common umbrella may lead to not only the end of diplomatic relations but may surely mean the end of the developmental pattern adopted and if the global legal order was to come into play, it would also help solve the capitalist-socialist divide as a law is there to be followed in both the systems and in that case the law will not create a problem of ideology.

But unfortunately, to oversee all this we have a study by the name global governance without global government and global law and many claims have emerged that the governance part can be legitimized by normative and sociological means which is a myth, as state consent and bureaucratization can never put forth a global democratic sphere without having a proper legal order.

The contention by some is also that a World tyranny may erupt after the Global Law comes into being but are national laws not in the same league or for that matter provincial and local law. Although the World government may have its takers and non-takers, the global law for the world may be very different in both practice and academia and it has to be there without a choice. But citizenship and boundaries are what seems to be the huddle for Global Law.

Now coming onto the self, the current phase of the society is such that people want the self and the internal democratic system of an individual as I call it is what the self-stands for and is different from the selfish dealing with the day to day things of daily routine but what I am forwarding is the fact that the self-needs to be based in between the globe and not on the basis of a map consisting of boundaries as that would not give even the self what he wants for the self and on the other hand, may not be able to put into effect the real will at play. But with this bipolar flux in the global law of the self and the overall mix, no middleman would prevail and this would help ensure a structured society at large. The Global Law would, in fact, swipe away the existing notions of nationality, class, sexuality, gender, and ethnicity which in the municipal sphere are in full swing. In fact, the global legal order would help solve two things; it would provide us with a world constitution or code of sorts and simultaneously would help elevate the individual code to never before seen heights. From where the individual and the globe would get attached in one string and as the institutions are being gobbled down by the national consensus models, similarly the diplomatic and the trade-related consensus which has erupted on major issues like expenditure, inter-national relations etc, is thus taking a hit due to the vagaries of the ionized contract.

The coming of such a law is even more important as under the onslaught of the forces of globalization and the emergence of centered steering by dominant states the need becomes even more important. And this global transformation gives space to the global law at large. In fact, it would be the homo-gene in the hetro-gene. As it can be very rightly said that the Nation-state is becoming obsolete and in this increasing scenario the insufficient Inter-national law shall be deleted in parts and the Global law should be placed on its behalf. As due to the inefficient Inter-national law we have seen weaker states losing influence in the International arena but also at their own national level which also is an important factor for bringing this legal order. The legislative aspect is also not in good plight, the UN which claims to be the sole legislative authority of the entire world is also missing the power and is frequently bypassed by bi-lateral and multi-lateral structures like the ASEAN or the NAFTA or even the WTO for that matter.

If sovereignty is the supreme power then the world should be that rather than a nation-state, as it is in itself an end to the shared norm of delivering necessities. Why can't the doctrine of jus cogens (literally higher law) be there for Global Law by which it overrides inter-national law as the latter itself uses to override domestic law, then the principle would be helpful in formulating a world legislative or say a global executive and judiciary which can make the enactments work, which is not there in say the Inter-national law as it lacks a common legislative and executive plus a proper working judiciary.

The great view of a multi-layered society is that it incircles on individual identity and upon a community, region, city, and the world. And if this world criterion is overlooked then its criteria is over, and it may be difficult to swipe away the inter-national conflicts. If the principle of individualism which collectively makes communitarianism which when further coagulated with others leads to nationalism and when another nation or a set of nations is added leads to inter-nationalism which lastly ends up on globalism, then why have disparity on laws which in the acute sense is not the globe. The relationship between individualism and globalism forwards the concept of the common good at the grass root and at the alba-trophic level.

Nations look for countries because in some deep sense they already have countries: the link between people and land is a crucial feature of national identity[1], the need erupts as inclusion was the problem even in Ancient Athens, regarded as the first great democracy it had the problem where women, slaves, and aliens were not at all given the right of citizenship and even Switzerland for that matter gave voting rights to women in 1971, A global law, in fact, would act as bridge between the nation, continent as well as lead to the incubation of the desired output.

World Courts can implement Global laws with the power to declare, clarify and revise statutes which would unambiguously apply to all of the territories of various nation-states. And mind you the Global Law can never be an agent of revolutions as they are full of self-interests and obsessions but by being the agent of the expression of belief it can fulfill the interests of all the factions. The other reasons for having a regime like this is that dominant players are playing cat and mouse with the minor players by using globalization as a tool, by forwarding open trade with all but when it comes to their own country of origin they start using protectionist measures like USA's 'Buy American'[2] and India's 'Swadeshi hi Sahi' propaganda's.

---

[1] Walzer, Michael (1996) "Spheres of Affection" In Joshna Cohen, ed., For the Love of Country (Boston: Becon Press). 125–127

[2] Anderlini, Jamil. 2009 "Buy China's policy set to raise tensions. Finacial Times, June 16.

If deliberative democracy can prevail at the national level then why can't at the global level. The divine agenda on economic, political and military parameters need to go in order to get a pure democracy but on the contrary a democratic society cannot succeed without such agendas at the municipal level, since there will be nothing to hold citizens together or to make them feel that they are engaged in a common political enterprise. Deliberate democracies at the regional level may create problems which the one global platform setup may solve.

And in this changing pattern of stratification where region, ethnicity, colour are again and again creeping up this mentioned order will deal with the said crisis, leading to the annihilation of class and cultural barriers. The long-term agenda of the world is to socially, economically, technologically advance but through this current trend and legal setup at a place, this may not at all be possible. It also cannot be denied that the nation-state is the centre stage of the modern era but the negative impact of the nation-state is nationalism which as an ideology may have been useful earlier but it now is losing its significance in this globalized era. Citing movements in Scotland, Catalonia and Kashmir can be said that nationalism is very much a mild ideology. But many don't even see it as a full-fledged ideology at all, mostly see it rather as a "thin-centered ideology which only has force when carried by other vessels" (Freedess, 1988).

On the other hand, Globalism is a dominant and powerful ideology of our time, which presents the globe as the inexorable and unavoidable fate of all nations, but unless a global legal order is brought this may not become a reality in the acute sense. One also needs to understand that without the annihilation of the nationalist ideology this may not be possible as the world ought to go to the post-ideological stage. As what is happening currently in say USA, India, France, UK, Germany is what will lead to the disorientation.

Globalism which will lead people to expand the conception might as well face the challenges of identity politics, also leading to the eruption of parochial identities and if the debate is forwarded that the nation-state came first and the national laws are of the topmost priority, then one needs to understand that the globalization story began much before the birth of nationalism and it began with the biological emergence of a very small number of our human ancestors who walked out of Africa and whose descendants reached every continent of the world.

The mentioned order is one which can relate the small little village to a large and humongous city. In fact, the law does not arise by the constitution of one state as the constitution is different in every subsequent state. But in fact, the law arises, historically in the limited horizon of the diverse "local villages".

Conclusion

In the end, all this boils down to the catastrophic globalized dispute between Human Rights and National Sovereignty. But with the globalization of markets, the inter-trend is failing and an engine for the globalization of law seems to be the only way out. No longer do we live in the world of discrete national communities. Instead, we live in a world where communities overlap each other on various strands.

Globalization can no longer be seen as an economic aspect as it carries with it the backing law and justice. Although Inter-national law has been there, its power in the International setup may very well be minimal and so the global law is what the circumference demands. The modern state is just run by laws framed by the parliament or the monarchy and the law is different in each and every one of them, and thus tensions also creep up on all aspects in that regard. And if the state and its laws are universal, then why can't the state coincide with other states in both policies and laws and this combination will only lead to a universal bond.

This is the question which the global law answers, the political relations that have arisen due to this international law has led to a threatening relationship where people get divided on the basis of their status in the state, relationship status with the other states and the economic status simultaneously are affecting the whole world order and except for the integration, it is causing a disintegration of sorts. The modern state was not regarded as deriving its sovereignty from the people, not even from God, at the same time the people are a particular set of beings, often seen as the members of the civil society which the state ruled, and then came in nationalism which setup political opposition and with it came in movements of unification and separation and then violence and disputes which led to the formulation of Inter-national law to dilute these disputes, then came in the multi-national disputes and trans-national uprisings but no law is there to tackle that core ingredient, People cannot deny the fact that this globalization needs to be elevated by a global law under the ruling of a global agency and automatic compliance of the law by the states and if there is violation then automatic action should be taken setting aside the fact as to whether the state is a developed one or an underdeveloped one.

Global Legal Order is thus the need of the hour...

REFERENCES

Limbic: An alternative to the left, right & centre [De facto Emotional Framework]

- *Schwarzmantel, J., 2008. Ideology and Politics. Okas, CA. Sage.*

- *Garner, Howard., 2006. Changing Minds: The Art And Science of Changing Our Own And Other People's Minds (Harvard Business School)*

Global Legal Order (Mankind in search of a Global Law) [De jure Legal Framework]

- Montevideo Convention on the rights and duties of states (Signed at Montevideo, 26th December 1933, entered into force 26th December 1934)

- Vogel, R. (1947) World Government. The Antioch Review, Vol. 7, No. 2 317-318. Available from: http://www.jstor.org/stable/4609217 [Accessed 24-01-2018].

- Conner, B., Tillett, C., R, J., Holman, Frank. (1947) Forum on World Government. Proceedings of the Section of International and

- Comparative Law (American Bar Association) 18-35. Available from: http://www.jstor.org/stable/25742751 [Accessed 24-01-2018].

- Hoss, G. (1905) A World-Government - World Peace. The Advocate of Peace (1894-1920), Vol.67, No.2.39-41. Available from: http://www.jstor.org/stable/25752458 [Accessed: 24-01-2018].

- Yunker, J. (2000) Rethinking World Government - A New Approach. International Journal on World Peace, Vol. 17, No. 1.2-33. Available from: http://www.jstor.org/ stable/20753240 [Accessed: 24-01-2018]

- Blanke, T. (1999) Local Village and Global Law. Available from: http://www.jstor.org/stable/24000929 [Accessed: 03-02-18]

- Thomas Blanke, Kritische Justiz, Vol. 32, No. 1 (1999), pp. 123-126. Stable (Accessed: 03-02-2018)

- Dean, M. (2007) Governing Societies: Political perspectives on the domestic and International rule, Maidenhead, England. Open University Press. 60-77

- Weale, A . (2007) Democracy, Basingstoke, United Kingdom. Palgrave Macmillan. 202-220

- Flynn, I . (2006) Deliberative Democracy and Divided Societies, Basingstoke, United Kingdom. Palgrave Macmillan.

- Kohli, A . (1990) Democracy & Discontent, Cambridge, United Kingdom. Cambridge University Press.

- Held., David., Mc Grew, A., Goldblatt, D., Perraton, J., 1999. Global Transformations: Politics, Economics and Culture, Stanford, CA. Stanford University Press. 103-118

- Couture, J ., Nielson, K., Seymous, M., 2000. Rethinking Nationalism. Canadian Journal of Philosophy Supplementary Vol 22

- Schwarzmantel, J., 2008. Ideology and Politics. Okas, CA. Sage.

- Ferguson, Yale ., Mansbach., Richard., 2012. Globalization. Abingdon, Oxon. Routledge

- Spencer, Philip., Wollman, Howard.,2005. Nations and Nationalism- A reader (Edited book). George Square, Edinburgh. Edinburgh University Press (Ch 5 Nationalism and the state- John Brevilly, Pg 61-74)

- Yeates, Nicola., Holden, Chris.,2009. The Global Social Policy Reader(Edited book). Polity Press

- Buchanan, A., & Keohane, R. (2006). The Legitimacy of Global Governance Institutions. *Ethics & International Affairs, 20*(4), 405-437.